Baby Animals of the Forest

by Michéle Dufresne

Pioneer Valley Educational Press, Inc.

I live in a tree. I have a big head.
I have feathers around my big eyes.
I have sharp claws on my feet.
I have a sharp beak.

Who is my mother?

My mother is an owl, and I am an owlet.

I was born without fur,
but I will grow a furry coat.
I drink my mother's milk.
I sleep in the winter. I like to swim,
and I like to climb trees.

Who is my mother?

My mother is a bear,
and I am a bear cub.

I have a mask around my eyes.
I sit on my back legs.
I can hold things with my
front paws. I am a nocturnal animal.
I am awake at night.

Who is my mother?

My mother is a raccoon,
and I am a baby raccoon.

I am black, and I have a white
stripe down my back.
If I am afraid, I might spray you!
I like to eat vegetables,
insects, and sometimes garbage.

Who is my mother?

My mother is a skunk,
and I am a baby skunk.

I have brown fur with white spots.
I drink my mother's milk.
My mother hides me in tall grass.
I stay with my mother
for one year.

Who is my mother?

My mother is a deer,
and I am a baby deer.
I am called a fawn.